REWARDING
TEAMS

MICHAEL ARMSTRONG

INSTITUTE OF PERSONNEL AND DEVELOPMENT

First published in 2000

Design and typesetting by
Wyvern 21, Bristol

Printed in Great Britain by
the Short Run Press, Exeter

British Library Cataloguing in Publication Data
A catalogue record for this book is available
from the British Library

ISBN 0-85292-860-2

i)

INSTITUTE OF PERSONNEL
AND DEVELOPMENT

IPD House, Camp Road, Wimbledon, London SW19 4UX
Tel: 020-8971-9000   Fax: 020-8263-3333
Registered office as above. Registered Charity No. 1038333
A company limited by guarantee. Registered in England No. 2931892

Contents

Other titles in the series

Introduction

Team rewards consist of payments or non-financial rewards provided to members of a formally established team. They are linked to the performance of the team as a whole, and are awarded in addition to the individual pay received by each team member.

Continuing interest is being expressed in team pay and other forms of team reward. The primary reason for this is because it is seen by many as a means of supporting effective teamwork in a team-based organisation. It is also perceived as an alternative to performance-related pay, with its focus on individual rather than collective effort, and which has often failed to meet expectations. Team pay has become one of the four aspects of reward management that are currently attracting the most attention, the other three being competence-related pay, broad-banding and job family pay structures.

However, team pay may not always be appropriate, and it can be difficult to operate. The criteria for success (as set out in Chapter 6) are demanding, which explains why the number of organisations that have taken it up is quite small and why other forms of rewarding teams are often preferred.

The incidence of team pay

There is conflicting information on the incidence of team pay. Research conducted in 1995 by the Institute of Personnel and Development (Armstrong and Ryden, 1996) – covering 98 organisations in both the public and private sectors – established that 24 per cent had formal links between team performance and pay. The organisations operating team pay systems were mostly in the financial services, high tech and pharmaceutical industries. The following approaches were adopted by these organisations:

- team bonus or incentive schemes – 87 per cent
- team measures included in performance management assessments – 26 per cent
- skill-based or competence-based pay – 22 per cent
- shop-floor work-measured group incentive schemes – 4 per cent.

Over half (52 per cent) of respondents with team pay were confident that team pay had improved team performance, but only 22 per cent could quantify the performance increase.

Research conducted by the Institute of Employment Studies in 1994 (Thompson, 1995) found that around 40 per cent of the respondents had introduced formal initiatives to encourage teamworking but these tended to be organisation wide rather than for one specific occupational group.

However, a recent survey (IRS, 1999) of 226 private sector organisations established that only 4.4 per cent had team pay, although 7.5 per cent were considering its introduction.

The problem with all these surveys is that of defining 'team pay'. It is reasonably certain that the companies responding to the IRS survey were stating that they had team pay only when their schemes covered tightly defined work groups who were eligible for rewards based upon the performance of the team. Other definitions of team pay extend it to organisation-wide schemes such as gain-sharing and executive bonus schemes that are related to company financial results.

Whatever definition of team pay is used, it is clear that this is not an approach to reward that has yet achieved, or perhaps will ever achieve, the popularity of individual performance-related pay (58 per cent of the IRS respondents had such schemes). The simple explanation of this situation is that team pay is believed by organisations to be less appropriate, or more difficult to apply, than individual performance pay. It is also true that the situations in which team pay is applicable are likely to be less common.

Financial and non-financial rewards for teams

Team rewards can be provided by both financial and non-financial means. The latter, as described in Chapter 2, are regarded as very important and there are many situations when team rewards are best provided by non-financial means. Financial rewards, however, are attracting a lot of attention and there are many practical issues affecting their use. That is why this guide devotes more space to team pay than to the other forms of reward.

Why team rewards?

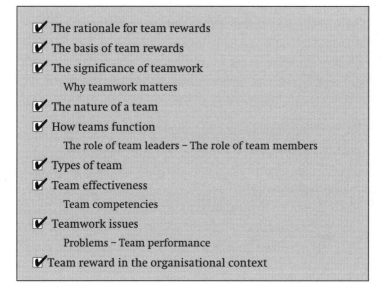

- ☑ The rationale for team rewards
- ☑ The basis of team rewards
- ☑ The significance of teamwork
    - Why teamwork matters
- ☑ The nature of a team
- ☑ How teams function
    - The role of team leaders – The role of team members
- ☑ Types of team
- ☑ Team effectiveness
    - Team competencies
- ☑ Teamwork issues
    - Problems – Team performance
- ☑ Team reward in the organisational context

The rationale for team rewards is discussed in the first section of this chapter. However, it needs to be considered against the background of an understanding of:

- the basis of team rewards
- the significance of team work
  and the issues that surround it
- how teams function, and therefore the basis upon
  which team rewards can be made

- the types of teams that exist for which targeted team rewards might be made available
- team effectiveness
- team reward in context

These matters are considered in later sections of the chapter.

The rationale for team rewards

The aim of team reward processes is to reinforce the behaviours that lead to and sustain effective teamwork. As claimed by Thompson (1995), team pay:

- rewards teamwork and co-operation
- encourages the group to improve work systems
- increases flexibility and the ability to respond to changing needs
- encourages information-sharing and communication
- helps to focus people on the wider organisation.

One of the most common reasons for developing team rewards is the perceived need to encourage group endeavour and co-operation rather than to concentrate only on individual performance. It is argued that pay systems for individual performance prejudice team performance in two ways. First, they encourage individuals to focus on their own interests rather than on those of their team. Second, they result in managers and team leaders treating their team members solely as individuals rather than relating to them in terms of what the team is there to do, and what they can do for the team.

The argument sounds convincing in organisations where teamworking is important, but it should not be taken too far. Members of teams still like to be treated as individuals. They may feel that they are contributing more than their fellow team workers and should be rewarded accordingly. From the viewpoint of the organisation it could be disadvantageous to neglect the impact of individual contributors. Insisting that the most important thing to be is 'a good team player' may inhibit individual initiative and innovation. Teamworking is a good thing, but so is independent judgement. This need not be incompatible with team membership, but it could be if there were too much emphasis on conformity within the group through the reward system.

The basis of team rewards

In a sense, all of us do what we are rewarded for doing, whether acting as individuals or as members of a team. When considering the introduction of team-based rewards there are two fundamental questions to be answered:

- Should teams be rewarded by financial means, by non-financial means or a combination of the two?
- To what extent can we rely on extrinsic (external) rewards, whether financial or non-financial, as distinct from intrinsic (internal) rewards?

The emphasis in team reward systems is usually on team pay rather than on other forms of non-financial rewards. Pay is, of course, important as a tangible means of recognition and reward and, in certain circumstances and within limits, as a motivator. That is why this good practice guide devotes a large portion of its contents to team pay.

7

However, the ultimate reward for teams, especially project teams, is often the successful accomplishment of a task, as long as that is recognised, and cash is not the only means of recognition. The choice is not between financial and non-financial rewards but between financial team rewards enhanced by non-financial rewards, and non-financial rewards alone. Worldwide research into team pay by the Motorola Corporation in 1994 found that in general their employees were more in favour of non-financial rewards than financial rewards for teamwork.

Teams, just like individuals, respond to both extrinsic and intrinsic rewards. Examples of extrinsic rewards are pay, bonuses, praise, public recognition and various forms of gifts. Examples of intrinsic rewards are satisfaction from accomplishing the team goals and a sense of well-being derived from strong work relationships, creative challenges, increased responsibility and learning opportunities.

The significance of teamwork

As Katzenbach and Smith (1993) emphasise: 'The primary purpose of top management is to focus on performance and the teams that will deliver it.' They also point out that teamwork represents a set of values that encourage behaviours such as listening and responding co-operatively to points of view expressed by others, giving others the benefit of the doubt, providing support to those who need it and recognising the interests and achievements of others. 'When practised, such values help us all to communicate and work more effectively together.'

The research for the IPD on the lean organisation as

reported by Kinnie and Purcell (1998) led to the following observations:

> Teamworking, it is claimed, can transform organisational performance and attitudes by creating a virtuous circle in which increased employee involvement leads to improved motivation and productivity.

According to Slater and West (1995):

> Teamwork enables people to accomplish more together than they would working alone and so, if successful, can be a source of satisfaction at work. In addition, team members can be supported by and learn from others, thus promoting personal and career development.

They mention that work relationships can contribute to the pressures of work, and they underline the importance of social support in teams as a means of improving team effectiveness by helping people to cope with work problems.

Why teamwork matters

It is generally accepted that teamwork matters more than ever before in the new de-layered, flexible, process-based and lean organisation. The following are the main factors influencing the drive for more effective teams:

- With fewer layers of management and a greater emphasis on horizontal processes, the requirement is for people to work more closely together in self-managed and cross-functional teams. As noted in the IRS *Employee Development Bulletin* (1995):

> The drastic reduction in layers of management in many organisations makes collaboration even more important and, in a slimmer organisation, the remaining sources of expertise relevant to a particular project or function must be brought together, rather than left scattered in isolated pockets throughout the depleted structure.

- Business process re-engineering is another factor leading to greater emphasis on teamwork. Process-based structures demand cross-functional working that only teams can facilitate, and such structures require a cultural shift on the part of employees, which may depend on teamworking.
- The drive for quality and customer focus. Total quality and customer care initiatives are often based on the development of improved teamwork.
- Technological change, often associated with the concept of the 'lean organisation'. A report by the Institute of Employment Studies – Giles *et al* (1997) – revealed that management structures designed in response to technological advances and competitive pressures are transforming the role of process workers. Many of the employers surveyed emphasised that teamworking in general, and cellular working in particular, entailed a move towards process operatives working on whole jobs, rather than on different tasks or components within jobs. Teams increasingly have responsibility for whole processes. In another

field, customer-focused organisations, especially
in the service industries, recognise the importance
of setting up teams that can concentrate on
improving levels of service for defined customer
groups.

- Interest in the concept of high-performance teams
which, as suggested by Katzenbach and Smith
(1993): 'Invest much time and effort exploring,
shaping and agreeing on a purpose that belongs to
them, both collectively and individually. They are
characterised by a deep sense of commitment to
their growth and success.' The members of high-
performance teams in the new organisation work
flexibly and are likely to be interdependent,
interchangeable, multi-skilled and jointly
accountable for results.

- The establishment in a few organisations of
largely self-managed or self-directed teams, which
consist of workers who are primarily related to
each other by way of task performance and task
interdependence. Self-managed teams are
allocated an overall task and given discretion over
how the work is to be done. Thus they plan,
schedule and control work and distribute tasks
themselves among their members. Team leaders,
if they exist, are working members of the team
whose main tasks are to provide guidance, help
and coaching as necessary, and to represent the
interests of the team to management and other
parts of the organisation.

The nature of a team

A team has been defined by Katzenbach and Smith (1993) as:

> A small number of people with complementary skills who are committed to a common purpose, performance goals and approach for which they hold themselves mutually accountable.

Katzenbach and Smith emphasise that the team is, or should be, a basic unit of performance in all organisations and that teams meld together the skills, experiences and insights of several people. They assert that: 'Teams outperform individuals acting alone or in large organisational groupings, especially when performance requires multiple skills, judgements and experiences.'

How teams function

Teams are concerned with task completion (results) and the building of relationships (process). Team rewards therefore need to recognise not only what the team has achieved (its outputs) but also how the results have been obtained (inputs).

Katzenbach and Smith point out that: 'Real teams develop when people work hard to overcome barriers that stand in the way of effective performance. By surmounting such obstacles together, people in teams build trust and confidence in each other's abilities.'

The role of team leaders

Team leaders traditionally clarify purpose and goals, ensure that team members are jointly committed to the achievement of these goals, strengthen the team's collective skills, monitor performance to ensure that targets are reached and provide positive feedback and recognition. They play an important part in the team reward process.

Although fully self-managed or self-directed teams are fairly rare, the traditional role of team leaders is being modified in many organisations. They are becoming less directive and more supportive of the team process. They provide guidance, help and feedback as necessary but act more as a part of the team, rather than as beings who lead a separate and superior existence.

The role of team members

Team members are concerned with three levels of performance:

- the actual role they carry out (their day-to-day world)
- the role they perform as team members
- the performance of the team as it affects the whole organisation.

Each of these levels needs to be considered when deciding how individual team members should be rewarded.

Types of team

The choice of team rewards will be influenced by the type of team. There are four categories:

- *Work teams* – these are self-contained and permanent teams whose members work closely together to deliver results in terms of output, the development of products or processes, or the delivery of services to customers. This type of team will be clearly focused on the achievement of a common purpose and its members will be interdependent – results are a function of the degree to which they can work well together. Team rewards may be appropriate for such teams as long as team targets can be established and team performance can be measured accurately and fairly.

- *Project teams* – these consist of people brought together from different functions to complete a task lasting from a few weeks to several years. After the project is completed the team often disbands. Examples include product-development teams or a team formed to open a new plant. Team rewards for project teams may be made as cash bonuses payable on satisfactorily completing the project to specification, on time and within the cost budget. Interim 'milestone' payments may be made when predetermined stages of the project have been completed satisfactorily.

- Ad hoc *teams* – these are functional or cross-functional teams set up to deal with an immediate problem. They are short lived and operate as a task force. It is unusual to pay bonuses to such teams unless they deliver exceptional results.

- *Organisational teams* – these consist of individuals who are linked together organisationally as members of, for example, the 'top management team', departmental heads in an operational or research division, section heads or team leaders in a department, or even people carrying out distinct and often separate functions, as long as they are all contributing to the achievement of the objectives of their department or section. Members of organisational teams can be associated with one another by the requirement to achieve an overall objective, but this may be loosely defined and the degree to which they act in consort will vary considerably. In a sense, organisations are entirely constructed of such 'teams', but team reward processes may be inappropriate unless their members are strongly united by a common purpose and are clearly interdependent. If this is not the case, some form of profit-sharing or gain-sharing (a formula-based scheme that enables employees to share with their employers' gains in added value) could be used to provide people with a share in the success of the organisation.

An alternative classification suggested by Gross (1995) lists the following types of teams:

- *Process or work teams* – full-time, permanent teams whose members work together to carry out a process.
- *Parallel teams* – part-time teams that meet to solve a particular problem and then disband, or that meet from time to time to deal with or monitor particular issues. They are often cross-functional.
- *Project or time-based teams* – full-time teams committed to completing a project within a given timescale and in which the membership may vary over time.

- *Hybrid teams* – teams that may have both full and part-time or rotating members.

Team effectiveness

Four factors that influence team performance were identified by Beckhard (1969):

- setting goals or priorities
- how work is allocated (roles)
- the way the team is working (its processes)
- the relationships between the people doing the work.

The essential characteristics of an effective team are that:

- it exists to attain a defined purpose and is successful in doing so
- members of the team are committed collectively and individually to achieving that purpose
- team members reinforce each other's intentions to pursue their team purpose irrespective of individual agendas.

As suggested by Lawler (1997):

> Team-based organisations work best if you get a collective sense of responsibility. You want your people saying, 'I'm responsible for what I do but I'm also responsible for what you do. And I need to encourage you; I need to criticise you if you're not doing anything.'

Team competencies

Hay/McBer competency research has found that teamwork and co-operation implies the intention to work co-operatively with others, as opposed to working separately or competitively. For this competency to be effective, the intention should be genuine. The core question is: *Does the person act to facilitate the operation of a team of which he or she is a member?* The generic Hay/McBer team competency scale, as quoted by Armstrong and Murlis (1998) contains the following five levels:

- *Co-operates*: Participates willingly – supports team decisions, is a good 'team player', does his or her share of work. As a member of a team, keeps other team members informed and up to date about the group process, individual actions, or influencing events; shares all relevant or useful information.
- *Expresses positive expectations*: Expresses positive expectations of others in terms of their abilities, expected contributions, etc; speaks of team members in positive terms. Shows respect for others' intelligence by appealing to reason.
- *Solicits inputs*: Genuinely values others' input and expertise; is willing to learn from others (including subordinates and peers). Solicits ideas and opinions to help form specific decisions or plans. Promotes team co-operation.
- *Encourages others*: Publicly credits others who have performed well.
- *Builds team spirit*: Acts to promote a friendly climate, good morale and co-operation (holds parties and get-togethers, creates symbols of group

identity). Resolves team conflicts. Protects/promotes group reputation with outsiders.

Teamwork issues

Teamwork, however, is not problem free, neither are teams necessarily more effective than people working individually.

Problems

As Kinnie and Purcell (1998) point out: 'Introducing teams can produce benefits, but there is a danger of creating a vicious circle in which repetitive and closely monitored work leads to low morale and poor performance.' They conclude that: 'Simply introducing teamworking does not in itself provide a solution to the problems created by supply-chain pressures. Successful teamworking depends on the basic principles of proper planning and communication, and on the necessary supporting HR policies and practices. In the absence of these, teamworking may result in the opposite of what it sets out to achieve.'

The full report on the IPD research into the lean organisation – Kinnie *et al* (1998) – produced other interesting findings on teamwork. The authors comment on the impact of teams as follows:

> Although there is clear evidence of an improvement in productivity, the improvements in participation are negligible; indeed, there is some evidence that teamworking reduces the quality of working life.

This, the researchers found, was partly attributable to the greater pressure to achieve tougher performance targets and the closer monitoring of both individual and group performance. As one manager said, work was now a combination of 'fun and surveillance'.

There is also an ethical issue about the use of teams. Companies may be keen about teams, especially self-directed ones, because they potentially do the work of managers for them. Team members can exercise social pressure on other members to conform to group norms, and if these are about increasing productivity in order to maximise team pay the pressure will be directed to those members who are seen as poor contributors. This could have desirable results – 'bringing the slackers up to scratch'. But it could be 'management by stress', applied by co-workers. This could well be accentuated if there are financial considerations, but is this desirable? It could be unfair as well as stressful and could obstruct any action that might be taken by or for individuals in this position to improve their performance.

Team performance

An overview of research on teamwork conducted by West and Slater (1995) led to the conclusion that teamwork can be difficult to achieve. They quote a number of research projects that showed that teams do not necessarily perform better than the aggregate of their individual members. The research indicates that the quality of the decision-making of the most able members is generally not matched by the overall decisions of the team, possibly because those with potentially excellent input into the decision-making process may be inhibited from putting their ideas forward, or their ideas may be ignored because they have lower status or are less dominant.

Team reward in the organisational context

It is individuals who receive team rewards. The total team reward system is built upon the foundation of the main element of reward – basic pay. It is necessary to get this right before considering any form of team pay. As reported in the IDS *Management Pay Review* (1993) some organisations, such as Ind Coope and Baxi Heating, see little need for team incentives. At both companies, team members are paid simple spot-rate basic salaries. Ind Coope believes that if all team members are on the same rate there are fewer arguments about who does what. Other companies, such as The Body Shop, recognise that flexible working, with team members sharing management responsibilities, implies greater pay equality. IDS also noted that teamworking is generating diverging pay strategies. On the one hand, there are those who are devising a range of incentive arrangements, team bonuses sometimes being coupled with individual performance-related pay. On the other hand, some companies are flattening pay differentials and placing little or no emphasis on incentive arrangements. According to IDS: 'It is the very novelty of trying to combine co-operative behaviour, group performance and a separate emphasis on individual contribution that has produced these conflicting approaches.'

Pay structures consisting of extended hierarchies are inappropriate in a teamworking environment. It is difficult to foster team spirit if members are concentrating on reaching the next rung on the promotion ladder rather than on improving team performance. Organisations like Glaxo Wellcome have introduced broad-banded structures (four or so bands covering the whole organisation) to encourage flexibility and teamworking.

Policies and practices on rewarding teams will be influenced strongly by the context of the organisation – its culture, structure, technology and competitive environment. That is why there is no such thing as 'best practice' in team rewards. What counts is 'best fit', and that is why there are many approaches to team reward, as described in the next chapter.

What types of team reward are available?

Team-based rewards defined

Team-based rewards are payments or non-financial rewards provided to members of a formally established team, which are linked to the performance of that team. Their purpose is to:

- encourage group effort and co-operation by providing incentives and means of recognising team achievements
- clarify what teams are expected to achieve by relating rewards to the attainment of predetermined and agreed targets and standards of performance, or to the satisfactory completion of a project or a stage of a project

23

- deliver the message that one of the organisation's core values is effective teamwork.

Types of team reward

As Lawler (1997) says, there are three approaches to team rewards: you can reward individuals for what they contribute to the team (the most common approach), you can reward the team as a whole for its performance, or you can pay them in accordance with the success of the business.

Team rewards, as defined above, are for collective effort and they may be financial or non-financial or a combination of the two. An individual can also be rewarded for working effectively as a team member. Teamworking may be one of the competencies that are reviewed in performance management processes, and individual performance-related pay or competence-related pay awards may take account of contributions to teamwork.

Financial rewards

Team-based financial rewards for work teams are shared among the team members in accordance with a published formula or on an *ad hoc* basis for achievements. This is what is often referred to as 'team-based pay' (described in Chapter 3) especially when it is applied to smallish permanent teams consisting of managers and staff. A distinction can be made between such a scheme and the other types of team or collective scheme, namely:

- rewards for project or *ad hoc* teams
- management team bonus schemes

- shop-floor group bonus schemes
- gain-sharing
- individual rewards for teamwork.

These are discussed in Chapter 4.

Non-financial team awards

Some people will agree with the view expressed by Coil and Frohman (1994) following their Motorola research, that:

> The most effective team rewards are a function of management and culture more than compensation, especially money. Support and recognition of team development and performance are more important to team members than team 'carrots'.

Financial rewards can act as incentives as long as teams are composed of people who are strongly motivated by money and who expect to receive a worthwhile financial reward as a result of the efforts of the team. But the motivational impact of money may not persist, and it may be diminished for individual team members because they find it hard to establish a line of sight between their behaviour and the reward. Some people may feel strongly that their pay should be related to their own efforts rather than being dependent on the performance of other people. For these reasons it may be undesirable to rely upon team pay alone, and consideration should be given to the other forms of non-financial extrinsic and intrinsic rewards that can be used specifically to supplement or even replace financial rewards.

Extrinsic non-financial rewards

The extrinsic non-financial rewards for teams are positive feedback, praise and recognition.

Positive feedback can be given formally at team review meetings by team leaders who itemise precisely what the team has achieved in each of its key performance areas. Praise from management or a team leader for work well done, or a notable accomplishment, can be part of a formal feedback process, but it can also be used less formally and more spontaneously during the everyday work of the team. As long as the praise is sincere and deserved it can have an immediate motivational effect.

Positive feedback and praise are both methods of recognition, but they can be even more effective if they are provided in writing, preferably by higher management. Greater impact will be made if the team's performance is recognised publicly in house magazines, on notice boards or at special events.

A tangible form of recognition which, while it costs the company money, is not strictly a financial reward, is to provide a special occasion for the team, such as a dinner, a trip to the theatre, or even a visit abroad to one of the company's overseas establishments. The team can also be called upon to represent the company or its business unit at outside or corporate events.

Intrinsic non-financial rewards

Intrinsic rewards are the self-generated factors that influence people to behave in a particular way or to move in a particular direction. For individuals, these factors include responsibility (feeling that the work is important and having control over one's own resources), a sense of accomplishment (recognition for oneself that something worthwhile has been achieved), a reasonable degree of freedom to act, the opportunity to influence events, scope to use skills and abilities, interesting and challenging work, opportunities for continuous development and membership of a supportive social group. These intrinsic motivators, which are concerned with what has been called 'the quality of working life' (a phrase and movement that emerged from this concept), are likely to have a deeper and longer-term effect because they are inherent in individuals and not imposed from outside.

The intrinsic motivators can work equally well in teams that feel they are accomplishing something worthwhile and have a proper degree of autonomy to manage their own affairs and to make operational decisions. Individual motivation will increase if team members believe they can exert more influence as part of a high-performance and self-directed team. Moreover, they may see more scope for personal growth in a team environment where the emphasis may be on flexibility and multi-skilling.

Providing non-financial rewards

Extrinsic rewards (eg public recognition) can be given by the organisation but will mainly be forthcoming from team leaders. Intrinsic motivation can be provided by increasing the degree to which teams are allowed to act autonomously.

Recognition can be provided in a number of ways:

- orally to the individual, immediately or at a performance review in which praise can be given

for a task well done or an important
accomplishment

- in writing to the individual – a personal note
  which may be recorded in the individual's file
- publicly, at a meeting, on a notice board or in a
  house journal
- by presenting a token gift at an event
- by giving some other voucher or gift.

Recognition is also provided by managers and team leaders who listen to, and act upon, the suggestions of their team members and, importantly, acknowledge their contribution. Other actions that provide recognition include promotion, allocation to a high-profile project, enlargement of the job to provide scope for more interesting and rewarding work, and various forms of status or esteem symbols. However, caution has to be exercised in the use of status symbols because they can be divisive. Virtually all informal rewards form a zero-sum game: one person's recognition also implies an element of non-recognition to others, and the consequences of having winners and losers, while almost inevitable, need to be carefully managed.

The research conducted by Coil and Frohman at Motorola (1994) showed that the following team reward and recognition approaches could be used at each stage of a team's development:

> *Stage 1 – Definition*: reward and recognition that helps team members to become familiar with their assignment and goals and the challenge they have been given; also actions that help them to get better acquainted with one another and grasp the different skill-set requirements to support team performance.

Stage 2 – Support: the rewards should encourage team members to support one another and develop into a team with its own identity.

Stage 3 – Reinforcement: recognition acknowledges the progress (or lack of it) of the team and its members as it pursues its assignment. Informal and formal rewards that provide feedback and encouragement are the most effective.

Stage 4 – Celebration: reward and recognition acknowledge achievement by the team as a whole and its members (eg performance evaluation). There is a clear message that the team effort is appreciated and that its results will count. The acknowledgement of poor performance, if that is the case, is also important. However, the appropriate reward and recognition in previous stages should reduce the likelihood of poor performance.

How does team pay operate for work teams?

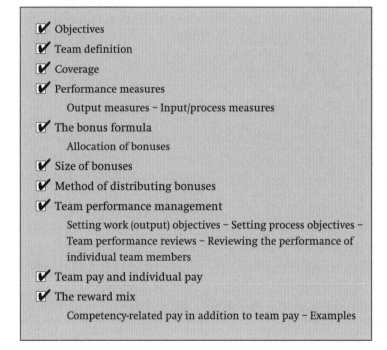

☑ Objectives
☑ Team definition
☑ Coverage
☑ Performance measures
  Output measures – Input/process measures
☑ The bonus formula
  Allocation of bonuses
☑ Size of bonuses
☑ Method of distributing bonuses
☑ Team performance management
  Setting work (output) objectives – Setting process objectives –
  Team performance reviews – Reviewing the performance of
  individual team members
☑ Team pay and individual pay
☑ The reward mix
  Competency-related pay in addition to team pay – Examples

A work-based team was defined in Chapter 1 as a self-contained and permanent team whose members work closely together to deliver results in terms of output, the development of products or processes, or the delivery of services to customers. This type of team will be clearly focused on the achievement of a common purpose and its members will be interdependent – results are a function of the degree to which they can work well together. Clear targets in such areas as output, productivity, sales, quality, speed of processing and response, and level of service to customers can be set for or by the teams and performance measures are available to management and team members to monitor progress and achievements against the targets.

Work team schemes relate bonus payments to the performance of a permanent work team. The features of such schemes are described below under the following headings:

- objectives
- team definition
- coverage in the organisation, ie the extent to which team pay applies
- performance measures
- the bonus formula – how bonus payments are made
- the size of bonuses
- how bonuses are distributed to team members
- team performance management
- rewards to individual team members
- the reward mix for work teams.

Objectives

The objectives set for team-based pay are usually concerned with improving performance by fostering and rewarding good teamwork. The team pay objectives of a manufacturing organisation quoted by Johnson (1996) were:

- to increase output per employee while reducing operating costs
- to encourage employee willingness to learn new skills
- to achieve more flexibility in employee work assignments
- to find a more motivating way to reward employees for productivity improvements than the existing profit-sharing plan.

The following are other examples of the objectives that organisations have set for team pay.

- *The Benefits Agency* – to give an increased emphasis to team performance, which is vital to the effective running of the Agency.

- *The Bradford & Bingley Building Society* (as reported by IDS, 1996) – to foster co-operation and teamwork between branches.

- *Coca Cola* – rewards in a teamworking environment should be:
  - team-oriented to support co-operation
  - competitive with appropriate peer groups
  - flexible, to address specific business needs
  - linked to business results
  - equitable in the treatment of associates
  - clearly communicated to all associates.

- *Hallmark Cards* – to focus team members on common goals and encourage them to exhibit behaviours that support the team more than individual objectives.

- *Norwich Union* – the team bonus scheme for financial planning consultants was introduced:
  - to achieve a cultural change in the direction of being more service-oriented
  - to ensure that consultants share best practice with their colleagues and provide help rather than competing on an individual basis.

- *Pacificorp* – to use team pay 'as a powerful communicator of values, directions and priorities'. Reward systems had to be linked to business strategy within a high-involvement workplace, where the emphasis was on flexibility and teamworking.

- *Pearl Assurance* – to encourage service staff to be more customer-focused and to meet the goals set by section managers.

- *Portsmouth Hospitals NHS Trust* – to encourage co-operation between individual directorates where clinical diversity may be perceived as goal diversity.

- *Trigon Blue Cross Shield* –
  - to create a 'triple win' – for customers, employees and the company
  - to enable the organisation to respond to customer needs more swiftly
  - to improve productivity and 'business literacy', ie understanding how teams contribute to business success

- to increase flexibility across the organisation and the ability to spread work resources.

● *Xerox UK* –
  - to encourage sales team members to co-operate, plan and make decisions together in working towards common goals and to minimise any internal competition ('portfolio' conflicts)
  - to support Xerox's strategic 'horizon' programme, which sees the company as a team working together in pursuit of a common goal
  - to ensure that employees encourage and coach each other to raise their performance, and are more willing to help their colleagues when help is needed.

Team definition

This type of team pay scheme has to be based on a precise definition of the teams to which it applies. When it comes to developing team pay one of the key decisions is the selection and composition of these teams. Certain criteria need to be met; they should:

● stand alone as performing units for which clear targets and standards can be agreed
● have a considerable degree of autonomy – team pay is likely to be most effective in self-managed teams
● be composed of people whose work is interdependent – it is acknowledged by members that the team will deliver the results expected of it only if they work well together and share the responsibility for success
● be stable – members are used to working with one

another, know what is expected of them by fellow
team members, and know where they stand in the
regard of those members

- be mature – teams are well established, used to
working flexibly to meet targets and deadlines,
and capable of making good use of the
complementary skills of their members
- be composed of individuals who are flexible,
multi-skilled and good team players while still being
capable of expressing a different point of view and
carrying that point if it is for the good of the team.

Coverage

It is sometimes assumed, wrongly, that team pay can be
introduced only if it covers every work team in the organisation. But if this course were pursued it would probably
end in disaster. The Coventry Building Society started to
develop team pay on this basis and soon found that it was
impracticable. They therefore limited its application to certain groups, such as branch staff. At Pearl Assurance, team
pay is restricted to sections of between 10 and 20 people in
the policy processing and claims areas, where around 1,500
staff are doing basically the same job. The customers for
these areas are primarily the sales agents in the field and
the level of service to these customers and their satisfaction
are critical soft measures of team performance in addition
to the hard measures of speed and accuracy of processing.

The reason for the limited take-up of team pay is simply
because there are few organisations in which everyone
employed could be fitted into teams that meet the exacting
criteria listed above. And to attempt to 'shoehorn' other

categories of staff into team pay schemes would prejudice the whole process. A further associated cause is the perceived problem of having different forms of pay schemes in one organisation – team pay for some but not for all employees.

The fact remains that the majority of companies with team pay for work groups have limited it to selected teams. This means that alternative rewards for those not in receipt of team pay have to be considered. Typically, these are provided in the form of individual performance-related pay and/or a company-wide bonus scheme, such as gain-sharing.

Performance measures

The performance criteria used as a basis for monitoring the performance of teams can be any one, or a combination of two or more, of the following output or input/process measures:

Output measures

- *Achievement of team goals* – results compared with targets; level of activity, speed of response or processing, efficiency, and the achievement of specified levels of accuracy, quality or customer service
- *Quantity of work* – output or productivity compared with targets/standards
- *Achievement of financial targets* – earnings, contribution, or net profit generated by team effort against targets
- *Customer satisfaction* – the degree to which standards for meeting customer expectations have been met as measured by such criteria as

customer satisfaction surveys, analysis of response and delivery times, complaints, and mystery shopping

- *Quality of work* – performance in meeting quality standards and specifications; evidence of continuous improvement; accuracy of work
- *Process knowledge* – extent of the job knowledge and technical or professional skill possessed and deployed effectively by the team in achieving results
- *Use and maintenance of technical systems* – capacity of the team to use and maintain technical systems
- *Flexibility* – ability of the team to operate flexibly in response to changing situations and demands; degree to which multi-skilling is developed; extent to which team members can be substituted for one another.

Input/process measures

- *Support of team process* – the degree to which the team is cohesive and members support and assist one another, even under pressure
- *Level of co-operative effort* – the extent to which team members work effectively together
- *Planning and goal-setting* – use of proactive planning and goal-setting to achieve results
- *Participative decision-making* – effort to establish jointly agreed courses of action
- *Communication* – use of open, honest and direct communication
- *Management skills* – ability to demonstrate such skills as budgeting, project management and monitoring performance.

The selection of performance measures will of course depend on the type of team, its activities and its overall purpose – what it is there to do. The selection will be influenced by an analysis of the critical success factors that apply to the team. A critical success factor describes what has to be done by the team to ensure that it achieves its goals. It indicates the key issues that the team has to address, and refers to the actions and behaviour that will make the difference between successful and unsuccessful performance.

When selecting performance measures it is useful to remember the advice given by Johnson (1996) on the basis of experience in introducing team pay into a number of US organisations. He commented that:

> Any chosen methods [of measuring performance] had to conform to four criteria: they had to (1) have business value; (2) be capable of being accurately and regularly measured and recorded; (3) be subject to direct or strong indirect influence by employees; and (4) be readily communicated to and understood by those employees eligible for the incentives.

But, as Pascarella (1997) suggests, measurement can be difficult: 'If it is not something that is easily measured, then you tend to measure an activity. Did you meet a milestone? Did you get it done? But that is harder to do. It just may be a candidate for after-the-fact recognition rather than project team incentives.'

It is necessary to ensure, so far as possible, that whatever measures are selected meet the following criteria:

- The measures are appropriate – they are aligned to the function of the team and its critical success factors.

- Reliable data will be available to establish levels of performance against the measure.
- Teams and their members will be able to track their performance against the measures.
- There is a clear line of sight between the levels of output and/or input and the bonuses that teams can earn; in other words, there must be an easily recognised relationship between performance (effort and contribution) and reward.
- The team accepts and understands the measures – this means that they must be given the opportunity to contribute to decisions on their selection and how they will be used.

The following are examples of the measures or criteria used by organisations.

- *The Automobile Association Scottish Finance Division* – teams are rewarded for their performance against productivity targets. This measurement is possible because the function is primarily a processing department with high volume, routine tasks to perform. An appropriate quality measure is also set by management.

- *The Benefits Agency* – bonuses are awarded to teams according to the key criterion that there has been 'a valuable contribution to performance'. Local criteria must be clear and published in advance, and payments can be made only if these predetermined criteria have demonstrably been met. In the case of the recognition payment as an incentive, a written agreement is normally drawn

up between the local unit manager and the team members. This makes clear:
- what the task is
- the standard to which it must be performed
- the timescale for completion
- the level of reward that will be made if the required standard is delivered.

- *The Bradford & Bingley Building Society* (as reported by IDS, 1996) – branch sales targets are set for lending, retail investment, the sale of regulated products and other commission-earning products. In addition there are four non-sales target areas:
  - branch costs
  - lending quality (risks incurred)
  - customer service as assessed by 'mystery shopping'
  - administration, covering customer complaints, adherence to customer service standards and the accuracy of financial and other returns to head office.

- *Coventry Building Society* – the measures for the branch network are net retail receipts, mortgage advances and insurance sales.

- *Dartford Borough Council* – each team has a series of targets. These are defined as tasks that:
  - are suitable for all or most of the team to undertake together
  - when successfully accomplished, will benefit the directorate/division and improve the performance and motivation of staff
  - are distinct from the tasks and activities set for

each team member as part of his or her normal duties as included in their job description.

- *Lloyds Bank* – team bonuses are payable quarterly to individuals on the basis of bank performance in relation to two 'challenges': the *Service Challenge* which is related to a service quality index, and the *Sales Challenge* which is linked to branch sales achievement against target. Considerable importance is attached to the service challenge because, as the bank states: 'Improving customer service continues to be a priority.'

- *Norwich Union* – the team bonus for financial service consultants is related to appointments attended, customer questionnaires completed and cases issued.

- *Pacificorp* – team results are based on two key measures:
  - the level of customer service as given by customer service and monitoring telephone calls
  - call availability – how frequently employees are available to answer telephones.

- *Pearl Assurance* – the 'hard' measures used for the customer service teams are speed and accuracy of processing; the 'soft' measures are levels of customer service.

- *Xerox UK* – recognising the need to develop a relatively simple system which would be readily understood by its employees, Xerox deliberately limited the number of the metrics feeding into the bonus calculation to three – customer satisfaction, sales revenue and market share. Each metric is measured regularly, with the results being relayed back to the individual teams.

The bonus formula

Bonus formulae relate the amount payable to individual team members to one or more measures of team perform-ance, or to the achievement of specifically agreed team objectives. There are a number of different approaches and the choice will depend on factors such as the type of team, the performance measures used and policies on how team bonuses should be distributed. The three basic approaches are these:

- *Performance related to defined criteria*, as at Lloyds Bank, Norwich Union and Pearl Assurance.
- *Bonus related to an overall criterion*, as at the Benefits Agency, where team bonuses are paid if there has been 'a valuable contribution to performance as determined by local unit managers'.
- *Bonus related to the achievement of predetermined organisational and team objectives*, as at Xerox, where they are linked to key organisational objectives. At Portsmouth Hospitals NHS Trust the bonus for directors and senior managers is based on an assessment of the Trust's success in meeting its corporate objectives.

The following are some examples of formulae.

- *Dartford Borough Council* – the targets can range in number from five to 20 but the norm is from six to

43

eight. All employees are members of a team, and
some are members of more than one team. For
example, a departmental manager will be part of the
management team and also part of the department
team. Each team has a series of targets. These are
defined as tasks that:

- are suitable for all or most of the team to
  undertake together
- when successfully accomplished, will benefit the
  directorate/division and improve the performance
  and motivation of staff
- are distinct from the tasks and activities set for
  each team member as part of his or her normal
  duties as set out in their job description.

Targets are allocated by the team manager after
consultation with the team members. They must be
consistent with the council's overall targets as
defined by the policy committee and cascaded down
through the directors. Each target must have a
measurable outcome in terms of performance,
including quality. They must also be time based. The
set of targets is required to involve the whole team in
an even and fair way so that all members can
contribute.

At the end of the year, the achievement of each
team in meeting its targets is assessed by two
measures. First, how has the team performed in
quality terms in its motivation to reach its targets, as
measured on a scale of one to six. Second, *how many*
of the targets have been reached in percentage terms.
These two measures are put together on a team

bonus matrix to define the provisional PRP team percentage increase, which is based on the minimum rate of pay in the grades of the individual team members. For individuals in two or more teams, a calculation is made which takes into account the agreed proportion of time spent in each team. The judgement of both these measures arises from an initial assessment by the team and its manager, followed by an appraisal by the senior manager/director. All of the provisional results are reviewed by the senior management team to reduce anomalies and inconsistencies.

- *Lloyds Bank* – payment is related to the 'service challenge' and the 'sales challenge'.

  The service challenge is defined by the service quality index (SQI), which governs rewards. It is based on the following weighted data:

	Weighting %
Customer view (questionnaire to existing customers)	45
First impressions (questionnaire to new customers)	15
Business customer view (questionnaire to business customers)	5
Telephone mystery shopping	15
Face-to-face mystery shopping	20
	100

Broad improvement targets are set on an SQI base for the previous quarter and are calculated by taking a percentage of the difference between the bank's SQI base and 100 per cent – this is called the improvement gap. The reward levels are related to branch targets for increasing their SQI.

The sales challenge operates on the basis of achievement against targets that generate *award units*. The three sales challenge groups are financial services and other operating income, new/converted accounts, and national products. Award units are allocated under each of these headings and the levels of reward are determined accordingly. The main benefit arising from the scheme is that it has focused the attention of branch staff on to the things that matter – sales *and* customer service.

- *Pearl Assurance* – the team-pay process starts by section heads meeting together at the start of the pay round and ranking the performance of each section by reference to the tangible performance measures. They then ask if it feels fair in relation to the softer measures before finally deciding on a rank order.

  The sections are then weighted. The top section is scored at 10 points. The next section down is scored in relation to the top section, and so on, to provide the measure of differentiation between the respective levels of performance between the sections. A computer model is used to determine a standard performance rating and a standard performance pay increase for each section. The model also supports levels of increase, if any, for performance in excess of or below standard. Each section manager then reviews individual performance directly with each member of staff, but within the context of the team's performance. The manager distributes the review fund using the computer model not as a rule but as a guideline.

- *Xerox UK* – the team bonus is based on the regional business plan and is determined by the team's performance against both the team revenue target and market share, with a multiplier for customer satisfaction performance. The current scheme also has a 'cumulative catch-up' built into it, which takes sales cycles into account.

Allocation of bonuses

Normally decisions on bonuses will be made by management by reference to performance against targets and standards, and on the advice of the team leader or departmental manager. According to Lawler (1997): 'Teams perform best when the head of the team has reward power over members for the time they work together.' But note can be taken of peer reviews, and a few organisations go so far as to get the team to decide on the distribution of bonuses.

Size of bonuses

A distinction should be made between bonus payments as incentives (ie to motivate better performance) and bonus payments as rewards (ie to recognise accomplishment).

To be effective as an incentive, bonuses have not only to be achievable but also worth having. It has been suggested by Lawler (1971) that a potential bonus of between 10 per cent and 15 per cent is probably required to provide motivation. As Gross (1995) points out:

> The key is to create a plan which equitably shares risk, offers a potential gain that makes the risk worth taking, and gives employees a fair chance of making more by working harder, smarter and better. It is necessary to find the right amount of pay at risk so that employees on the team feel adequately rewarded when the team performs adequately, but can feel handsomely rewarded when performance soars.

The amount and method of distribution of team pay varies considerably in practice, for example:

- *The Automobile Association* – teams in Scotland selling financial services can receive payments in vouchers to the annual value of 4 per cent of basic salary, and sales teams selling membership to fleet operators can receive about 8 per cent. Team leaders and team managers of member recruitment teams can receive rewards for team sales performance worth about 8 per cent of basic salary – the staff actually making the sales are rewarded individually.
- *The Benefits Agency* – recognition awards are made as non-consolidated lump sums in cash. There is no upper or lower limit for the level or the number of awards that can be made to a team, although the maximum amount that could be set aside for the recognition scheme in 1994/95 was 0.5 per cent of the staff paybill for each unit, and awards totalling over £1,000 to an individual in any one year have to be referred to the area director for clearance. The

recognition scheme can also be used to reward individuals for specific and well-defined cases of personal achievement, but it is designed to supplement individual merit pay and will not be paid for achievements already covered by the normal performance appraisal and merit pay scheme.

- *The Bradford & Bingley Building Society* – a quarterly team bonus of 5 per cent is paid to branch staff for on-target sales.
- *The Coventry Building Society* – annual payments are made to teams, which are based on performances related to target in accordance with a scale capped at 15 per cent above the target rate. For example, the target performance in 1998 was 7 per cent and the branch network teams received a median bonus of 8.47 per cent of the base salary of team members.
- *Dartford Borough Council* – the average team award in 1995 was 5 per cent of their pay.
- *Hallmark Cards* – performance team pay for managers and staff is 10 per cent of fixed pay.
- *Lloyds Bank* – in 1995, the quarterly payment to team members was set at a maximum of £400.
- *Trigon Blue Cross Shield* – the introduction of team-based pay involved 'putting more pay at risk' by reducing base salaries and individual merit awards. In return, teams were given the opportunity to earn incentives worth up to 15 per cent of salary.
- *Xerox UK Limited* – members of sales teams in 1995 could earn a bonus of £3,500.

Method of distributing bonuses

Bonuses can be distributed to team members in the form of either the same sum for each member, often based on a scale of payments, as at Lloyds Bank and Norwich Union, or as a percentage of base salary, as at the AA, the Benefits Agency, Dartford Borough Council, Pearl Assurance and Portsmouth Hospitals NHS Trust.

Payment of bonus as a percentage of base salary is the most popular approach. The assumption behind this method is that base salary reflects the value of the individual's contribution to the team. The correctness of this assumption clearly depends on the extent to which base salary truly indicates the level of performance and competence of individuals as team members.

Payment of the same fixed bonus to all team members reflects the view that all team members should be rewarded equally for their collective efforts. If the base salary is related to competence as a team member as well as an individual contributor then this approach is based on the belief that any differential in the contribution of team members has already been catered for.

Team performance management

Team pay works best if there are effective and accepted performance management processes for the team. Team performance management activities follow the same sequence as for individual performance management:

1 Agree objectives.
2 Formulate plans to achieve objectives.
3 Implement plans.

4 Monitor progress.

5 Review and assess achievement.

6 Redefine objectives and plans in the light of the review.

The aim should be to give teams with their team leaders the maximum amount of responsibility to carry out all activities. The focus should be on self-management and self-direction.

The key activities of setting work and process objectives and conducting team reviews and individual reviews are described below.

Setting work (output) objectives

Work or output objectives for teams will be based on an analysis of the purpose of the team and its accountabilities for achieving results. Targets and standards of performance should be discussed and agreed by the team as a whole. These may specify what individual members are expected to contribute. Project teams will agree project plans that define what has to be done, who does it, the standards expected and the timescale.

Setting process objectives

Process objectives are also best defined by the team getting together and agreeing how they should conduct themselves as a team under headings related to the list of team competencies and performance measures referred to earlier in this chapter, including:

- interpersonal relationships
- the quality of participation and collaborative effort and decision-making

- the team's relationships with internal and external customers
- the capacity of the team to plan and control its activities
- the ability of the team and its members to adapt to new demands and situations
- the flexibility with which the team operates
- the effectiveness with which individual skills are used
- the quality of communications within the team, and between the team and other teams or individuals.

Team performance reviews

Team performance review meetings analyse and assess feedback and control information on their joint achievements against objectives and project plans. The agenda for such meetings could be as follows:

1 *General feedback review*:
   - progress of the team as a whole
   - problems encountered by the team that have caused difficulties or hampered progress
   - helps and hindrances to the operation of the team.

2 *Work reviews*:
   - how well the team has functioned
   - review of the individual contribution made by each team member – ie peer review (see below)
   - discussion of any new problems encountered by individual team members.

3 *Group problem-solving*:
   - analysis of reasons for any shortfalls or other problems

- agreement of what needs to be done to solve them and prevent their reoccurrence.

4 *Update objectives*:
- review of new requirements, opportunities or threats
- amendment and updating of objectives and project plans.

Reviewing the performance of individual team members

Processes for managing team performance should not neglect the needs of team members. As Mohrman and Mohrman (1995) point out: 'Performance among individuals, teams and organisations need to fit, but individual needs must be met at the same time.' They ask how individual needs can be met while still encouraging the sharing required at the group level. Their answer is:

> First, teams have to be managed in a way that enables individuals to feel they can influence group performance. They must provide opportunities for involvement and for team self-management. Second, the team must be managed so that the individual's needs to have excellent performance recognised are met.

Individuals should receive feedback on their contribution to the team and recognition by their team leader and fellow team members for their accomplishments. Special attention should be given to their personal development, not only as members of their existing team, but also for any future roles they may assume in other teams, as individual contributors, or as team leaders.

Individuals should agree their objectives as team members with their team leader, but these can also be discussed at team meetings. Personal objectives and personal development plans can also be formulated for agreement with the team leader. Performance and development reviews between team leaders and individuals can concentrate on the latter's contribution to the team, the level of performance in terms of teamwork competencies, and progress in implementing personal development plans.

Peer review processes can also be used in which team members assess each other under headings such as:

- overall contribution to team performance
- contribution to planning, monitoring and team review activities
- maintaining relationships with other team members and internal/external customers
- communicating
- working flexibly (taking on different roles in the team as necessary)
- co-operation with other team members.

Peer reviews can form part of a 360-degree feedback or multi-source performance management process. But as Jay Schuster (quoted in Pascarella, 1997) remarks:

> Team organisations are becoming more prevalent so the first thing to do is to base all team members' pay on team performance only. Most teams are not ready to base pay on multi-source performance management early in their formation. When the team becomes mature enough, the members will let you know they're ready to have pay based on

individual performance. The best way to do that is 360-degree performance management.

Team pay and individual pay

Two of the thornier team pay issues are first, whether the motivation of performance through individual rewards will be more effective than motivating people collectively through team rewards, and second, the degree to which individual members of teams in receipt of team pay should be rewarded in relation to their performance, competence and contribution. It can be contended, as does Pascarella (1997) that rewards should be tailored to the individual on the assumptions that:

- motivation comes from the individual, not the group
- the development of skills and behaviours is an individual undertaking
- fairness in dealing with teams does not mean equal pay for all
- expressing oneself within the context of co-operation is replacing wild notions of individualistic behaviour
- team compensation is not a payoff but a means of nurturing behaviour that benefits the group.

These arguments are powerful enough to deter many organisations that believe in encouraging and rewarding individual effort from adopting team pay. And as Pascalella also contends:

> Burying incentives recognition for team membership in the company's basic compensation package can dampen the intended motivating effect for

individuals, so look for ways to *add on* incentives and recognition for team participation.

Some organisations, such as Lloyds Bank and Portsmouth Hospitals NHS Trust, pay team bonuses only. Others, such as the Benefits Agency, Norwich Union and Pearl Assurance, pay both team and individual bonuses. It can be argued that people want to be rewarded for their individual contributions, but the problem with teams, as Gross (1995) says, 'is that it is really hard to separate out what any individual really contributes'.

The reward mix

As Gross (1995) suggests: 'For some teams a carefully crafted mix of individual and group incentives may be most appropriate.' The mix can consist of base pay plus one or more of the following:

- shared team bonus, as described above
- individual competency-related pay, as described below
- bonus based on organisational, functional or plant performance, for example gain-sharing, as described in the next chapter
- non-financial rewards, including recognition schemes, as discussed in Chapter 2.

Competency-related pay in addition to team pay

Competency-related pay is a method of rewarding people individually for what they contribute to the team. It can operate by relating base pay to the level of competency, and/or the degree to which an individual is multi-skilled and can therefore carry out some or all of the group's tasks.

The aim is to develop each team member so that he or she achieves the full level of competency as a contributor to the team's performance, and is also multi-skilled. All fully competent and flexible team members would receive the same base pay. An individual process of performance management will be necessary to assess competency. This could be done by the team leader, but a peer review by other members of the team is sometimes used. There are clearly some problems in getting team members to assess one another, but it can be argued that members of teams will know much more about each other's performance than anyone else.

Examples

An example of a company with a mixed pay package for team members is ESCA Corporation, an engineering firm in Washington, which uses a three-tier reward system. Part of the employee's pay is team based, part of it is organisationally based and part of it is based on individual achievement.

An example of a firm using competency-related pay for individuals is Pacificorp, as reported by IRS (1997a). Team pay is awarded as an additional bonus. Competency-related pay is defined as:

- pay for person (and competencies applied to work) versus job
- pay for many 'jobs' versus a specific job
- pay for learning and applying competencies to new jobs versus performance or seniority
- base pay increases or lump sums for utilised competencies.

There is a set of nine core competencies, six of which are

based on business processes: customer service requests, billing, credit and collections, energy efficiency, team skills and service management. The other three core competencies – business knowledge, technical skill and communications – are 'required and not paid for'.

The three competency levels are:

- contributor level – beyond entry-level training in each of the core competencies, which they are expected to achieve in a period of between six and 12 months
- 'pro' level – able to apply challenging competencies; a proficient, capable performer
- champion level – able to apply complex competencies; an expert role model.

The development of competencies depends on team needs.

How do other forms of
team pay work?

In this chapter alternative approaches to team pay are considered, as follows:

- team pay for project teams
- bonuses for groups of senior executives
- shop-floor group bonus schemes
- gain-sharing
- company or plant-wide bonus schemes
- rewarding individuals for effective teamwork.

Team pay for project teams

Project teams may receive after-the-event lump sum bonuses for achieving predetermined targets for completing the project to specification, within budget and on time. Stage payments are sometimes made when the team has reached defined milestones.

For example, IBM offers outsourcing services as part of its core business activities. The first stage of the outsourcing process involves an IBM engagement executive visiting potential customers in order to make an initial assessment of their requirements. The engagement executive then assembles a specially tailored 'bid team' consisting of a group drawn from IBM's various business units, which may include technical, personnel and legal experts. It is the bid team's responsibility to develop the best possible tender for the outsourcing contract. However, winning a contract with a customer involves a detailed and often protracted tendering process that may last years rather than months.

If IBM wins the contract, an award is made to members of the bid team in recognition of their contribution to the win. The engagement executive is responsible for rating contribution and presenting recommendations to the outsourcing management team.

The financial award is often allocated to members of the firm who are not usually involved in direct revenue generation, such as the legal advisers. The same bid team tends never to be assembled twice, so this reward mechanism enables IBM to reward a unique grouping of employees on a one-off basis for work that would not be rewarded as part of their normal base salary.

Bonus schemes for executive directors

Bonuses can be paid to the top team of executive directors based, usually, on the performance of the business as a whole, on the grounds that they are jointly accountable for that performance. Part of the bonus, however, may be related to the achievement of individual targets. Recent surveys have indicated that by far the most used performance criterion is pre-tax profit. The next most popular measure is earnings per share (profit after interest, taxation and ordinary dividends divided by the number of ordinary shares issued by the company), followed by return on capital employed, and then cash flow. Profit and earnings per share are the most common criteria used by analysts and the financial press to assess company performance.

Performance-related bonuses are related to the achievement of a target. This may simply be the profit target in the annual budget or the longer-term plan. An alternative method of setting a target is to relate it to a minimum level of improvement compared with the previous year or, if the previous year was a poor one, the highest level reached in the previous two or three years. This avoids setting the target at too low a figure.

Group incentive schemes for manual workers

Group incentive schemes provide for the payment of a bonus either equally or proportionately to workers within a group or area. The bonus is related to the output achieved over an agreed standard, or to the time saved on a job – the difference between allowed time and actual time. In the latter case, work measurement is used to determine times allowed.

Group bonus schemes are in some respects individual incentive schemes writ large – they have the same advantages and disadvantages as any payment-by-results system. The particular advantages of a group scheme are that it encourages team spirit, breaks down demarcation lines and enables the group to discipline itself in achieving targets. In addition, job satisfaction may be achieved through relating the group more closely to the complete operation. Group bonuses may be particularly useful where groups of workers are carrying out interdependent tasks and when individual bonus schemes might be invidious because workers will have only limited scope to control the level of their own output and will be expected to support others, to the detriment of their personal bonus.

The potential disadvantages of group bonus schemes are that management is less in control of production – the group can decide what earnings are to be achieved and can restrict output. Furthermore, the bonus can eventually cease to be an incentive. Some opponents of group schemes object to the elimination of personal incentive, but this objection would be valid only if it were possible to operate a satisfactory individual incentive scheme, which is not always the case.

Group schemes may be most appropriate where people have to work together and teamwork has to be encouraged. They are probably most effective if they are based on a system of measured or controlled daywork where targets and standards are agreed by the group, which is provided with the control information it needs to monitor its own performance.

The shop-floor team reward scheme developed by Ethicon, the surgical supplies manufacturer, as reported by IRS (1996a) was introduced to reinforce teamworking in order to improve productivity and the level of customer service, and also to provide for greater flexibility in its manufacturing operation and to support the new continuous-flow manufacturing process. A multi-factor team bonus scheme was installed to replace the existing individual incentive arrangements. The team bonus is linked to the following three key performance measures, each closely aligned to the company's business goals:

- output – which relates to the quantity of goods produced by the team
- quality – with a greater emphasis on quality assurance and employees auditing their own work
- lead time – the time it takes the product to complete the manufacturing process.

The bonus is divided equally between all the members of a team.

Gain-sharing

Gain-sharing is a formula-based company- or factory-wide bonus plan, which provides for employees to share in the financial gains made by a company as a result of its improved performance. A typical formula determines the share by reference to increases in added value. In some schemes the formula also incorporates performance measures relating to quality, customer service, delivery or cost reduction.

Fundamentally, the objective of gain-sharing is to

improve organisational performance by creating a motivated and committed workforce who want to be part of
a successful company. More specifically, as described by
Armstrong and Murlis (1998), the aims of gain-sharing are
to:

- establish and communicate clear performance and
  productivity targets
- encourage more objective and effective means of
  measuring organisational performance
- increase focus on performance improvement in the
  areas of productivity, quality, customer service,
  delivery and cost
- encourage employees to participate with
  management in the improvement of operating
  methods – one of the most important characteristics
  of an effective gain-sharing plan is that it
  incorporates arrangements for the joint discussion of
  methods of improving performance
- share a significant proportion of performance gains
  with the employees who have collectively
  contributed to improvements.

At BP Exploration (BPX), as reported by IRS (1996b), gain-
sharing involves paying employees a bonus for 'stretch performance beyond the business plan. These plans focus the
key performance measures: of production, cost and safety
with an additional element tied to the performance of the
company as a whole.' According to BPX, the scheme has:

- helped to align employees with performance targets
- increased staff participation and commitment
- enabled the company to reinforce its teamworking

arrangements by providing a direct link between business performance and team reward.

At Rank Xerox, as reported by IRS (1997b), the added value gain-sharing plan was defined as 'a scheme designed to encourage all employees across the site to participate and contribute in order to improve our competitive advantage and share the benefits'.

Company- or plant-wide bonus schemes

Gain-sharing divides the added value produced by the company and its employees between the company and employees in accordance with a predetermined formula and, ideally, includes employee involvement as a major feature of the plan. Company- or plant-wide schemes simply allocate cash bonuses by reference to plant or company performance in terms of output or productivity.

In British Steel, as reported by IRS (1998), an extensive programme for developing teams as part of a lean production approach has taken place. The incentive pay for team workers is based on the performance of the works or department. Known as the 'Works Quarterly Lump-sum Bonus Scheme', this can add up to 25 per cent of basic pay.

Rewarding individuals for effective teamworking

Individuals can be rewarded on the basis of assessments of their competency as teamworkers. Such awards may enhance basic pay for members of a work team receiving bonus payments. Alternatively, they could provide a method of recognising the teamworking skills of individuals even when there are no formal team pay arrangements.

Levels of competency under different headings could be expressed in behaviourally anchored rating scales, as in the example on the opposite page.

Such scales are best prepared in conjunction with team members. They should be asked what headings are appropriate, and be encouraged to supply definitions of different levels of performance based on their own experience, and expressed in their own language.

Example

At British Steel, payment for team workers consists of three elements: base pay, incentive pay as described earlier, and skills pay. The last is called the 'Personal Competency Supplement' and is determined by the accreditation of skills needed within the team. Significantly, however, the actual performance of teams does not influence pay. This is because team performance pay would be difficult to quantify and be potentially divisive in an environment where the emphasis is on the co-operation between different teams in the production process.

A behaviourally anchored rating scale

	Input to team	Team player	Team support	Multi-skilling	Quality of work	Customer care
1	Does more than his/her share of the work; makes an oustanding contribution to the team's performance.	Participates willingly; makes a major contribution to the team's decisions; supports agreed team decisions.	Behaviour makes a significant contribution to creating a friendly atmosphere; provides ample support to other team members; encourages others.	Fully flexible; capable of carrying out all the team's tasks.	Consistently delivers high quality and accurate work.	Consistently delivers high levels of customer service; responds quickly and helpfully to customer requests.
2	Does a reasonable share of the work of the team; makes an acceptable contribution to the teams performance.	On the whole, works well with other team members; makes an acceptable contribution to the team's decisions; generally supports agreed team decisions.	Behavior helps to create a friendly atmosphere; gives some support and encouragement to other team members.	Quite flexible; can carry out most of the team's tasks.	Achieves an acceptable standard of quality and accuracy.	Meets customer care standards; responds reasonably quickly and helpfully to customer requests.
3	Does not pull his/her weight; does not make an acceptable contribution to the team's performance.	Reluctant to join in; does not get on very well with other members of the team; does not make much of a contribution to team decisions and does not always support agreed decisions.	Behaviour can sometimes be unfriendly; gives little support or encouragement to other team members.	Somewhat inflexible; can carry out only one or two of the team's tasks.	Quality and accuracy of work not always up to standard.	Does not seem to be prepared to take a proper interest in customer service; response to requests neither as prompt as it should be nor particularly helpful.

What are the advantages and disadvantages of team pay?

Team pay may seem to be an attractive option, and there are many benefits it can provide. But there are also some formidable difficulties, which might explain why other ways of rewarding individuals are preferred by most organisations.

Advantages of team pay

Team pay can:

- encourage teamworking and co-operative behaviour
- clarify team goals and priorities and provide for the integration of organisational and team objectives
- reinforce organisational change in the direction of an

increased emphasis on teams in flatter and process-based organisations

● act as a lever for cultural change in the direction of, for example, quality and customer focus

● enhance flexible working within teams and encourage multi-skilling

● provide an incentive for the group collectively to improve performance and team process

● encourage less effective performers to improve in order to meet team standards

● serve as a means of developing self-managed or self-directed teams.

Disadvantages

The disadvantages of team pay are that:

● its effectiveness depends on the existence of well-defined and mature teams – but they may be difficult to identify and even if they can be, do they need to be motivated by a purely financial reward?

● team pay may seem illogical to individuals whose feelings of self-worth could be diminished – it is not always easy to get people to think of their performance in terms of how it impacts on other people

● distinguishing what individual team members contribute could be a problem – this may not be regarded as a disadvantage by a fervent believer in teams, but it might demotivate individual contributors who may still have much to offer, inside as well as outside a team setting

- peer pressure that compels individuals to conform to group norms could be undesirable – insistence on conformity can be oppressive
- pressure to conform could result in the team maintaining its output at lowest common denominator levels – sufficient to gain what is thought collectively to be a reasonable reward, but no more
- it can be difficult to develop performance measures and methods of rating team performance that are seen to be fair – team pay formulae could be based on arbitrary assumptions about the correct relationship between effort and reward
- problems of uncooperative behaviour may be shifted from individuals in teams to the relationship between teams
- organisational flexibility may be prejudiced – people in cohesive, high-performing and well-rewarded teams might be unwilling to move, and it could be difficult to reassign work between teams or to break up teams altogether in response to product-market or process developments, or to competitive pressures. And there may be pressure from those working in poor teams to migrate to good teams.

Conclusions

The case for team pay looks good in theory, but there are some formidable disadvantages. The criteria for success, as discussed in the next chapter, are exacting and it has not yet been proved that team pay for white-collar workers will inevitably be effective. Perhaps this is why, in the UK, team pay has been more talked-up than put into practice. This does not mean that team-based pay should be dismissed as yet another 'flavour of the month'. There a number of organisations mentioned in this guide that truly believe that it works well for them, even if they cannot always quantify the benefits. But there are powerful arguments against relying on team pay alone to transform the effectiveness of teams. The case for using non-financial means of rewarding teams to support team pay or, indeed, for relying on such means entirely, is a strong one.

What are the criteria for team pay?

☑ Core values and management style
☑ A climate of trust
☑ Requirements for team pay to act as an incentive

For team pay to be effective:

- it must be congruent with the organisation's core values and management style
- there should be a climate of trust in the organisation
- the characteristics of the teams themselves should be appropriate for team pay
- it should act as an incentive, or at least provide a worthwhile reward.

Core values and management style

For team pay to be congruent with the organisation's values the members of the top management team should believe that:

- good teamwork will make a significant contribution to competitive advantage and will create added value
- superior team performance deserves to be rewarded financially.

The management style should be one that is prepared to devolve authority to teams and to give them scope to manage themselves – if not entirely, at least to a reasonable degree.

A climate of trust

Team pay, like any other form of reward, works best if there is a climate of trust in the organisation: if employees trust the motives and declarations of intent of management; and if management trusts employees to play their part in making it work. As Thompson (1995) emphasises:

> For teams to prosper, individual team members need to believe that the team pay scheme is not there to exploit them, and that both team members and the organisation are going to benefit from collaboration.

Requirements for team pay to act as an incentive

Team pay may be valuable as a means of recognising achievement and indicating team priorities, but how effective can it be as a direct incentive? For team pay to function well as an incentive, 10 requirements need to be met:

- All the members of the team understand and accept the targets to be met – they should preferably be involved in agreeing those targets.

- The reward is clearly linked to the effort and achievements of the team – members' expectations are that high levels of performance or specified behaviours will lead to rewards.
- The reward is valuable enough to be worth striving for.
- Fair, consistent and acceptable means are available for measuring performance – you cannot pay for performance unless you can measure performance.
- Team members are able to use these measures to track their performance in relation to the agreed targets and standards.
- The team is able to influence its performance, and therefore the incentive payment, by changing its behaviour or decisions.
- The incentive or bonus formula is easy to understand.
- The reward follows as closely as possible the accomplishment that generated it.
- The scheme is appropriate to the type of team and the work it carries out.
- The scheme is carefully designed, installed, maintained and adapted to meet changing circumstances.

These are exacting requirements and organisations must be certain they can be met before introducing team pay. That is why team pay can be unsuccessful as a direct means of motivating superior team performance. For the same reason, individual performance-related pay schemes often fail to act as motivational devices.

Team pay may, however, be justified as a reward process that provides a tangible means of recognising the value of people. There are four reasons for considering team pay if the circumstances are favourable:

- It is just and equitable to reward people according to the contribution they make as team members or individuals – people should be paid for how well they perform.
- The organisation demonstrates that it values teams and individuals who perform well – and people can be motivated by knowing that they are valued.
- Team pay delivers the message that high levels of team performance are important.
- Attention can be focused on the aspects of performance to which priority should be given, and on the core values to be upheld in such areas as quality, customer service, innovation *and* teamwork.

How should team pay be introduced?

The steps required to introduce team pay are to:

1 analyse the situation and the requirements of the organisation
2 set objectives for team pay
3 consult with and involve employees
4 design the scheme
5 introduce the scheme
6 train teams and team leaders (as part of the introduction programme)

7   monitor and evaluate the scheme.

Analysis of the situation and requirements

The success of team pay depends upon the rigour with which initial analyses are conducted of the scope for introducing it and of the requirements of the organisation and its members. The analyses should cover:

1   *Team definition* – the aim of this analysis is to establish which teams might be eligible for team pay in terms of the characteristics required, as specified in Chapter 6. It would cover:

   – the types of teams in the organisation, analysed into the four main categories, ie work teams, project teams, *ad hoc* teams and organisational teams
   – the extent to which any of these teams are recognisable as clearly defined units that are required to deliver specified results
   – the degree to which members of these teams are interdependent and are required to be flexible and multi-skilled in achieving their team's purpose.

2   *Scope for team rewards* – on the basis of the team definition analysis, the scope for team pay should be considered in terms of:

   – the type of team pay that would be appropriate, eg team bonus schemes, gain-sharing or plant bonus plans
   – the likelihood that team pay would generally

improve teamworking and team performance in appropriate teams
- the use of non-financial means for rewarding teams
- the possibility of introducing competency in teamwork as a factor in performance management processes.

The results of the first two areas of analysis should indicate whether or not team pay is worth pursuing and, if so, the teams that might be included (which would not necessarily cover the whole organisation).

3   *Team behaviour* – the type of team and team member behaviour that the organisation wants to encourage through team reward processes. This could include:

- team direction – whether through an appointed team leader or by a process of self-management
- team commitment – the identification of individual team members with the team and to the achievement of its purpose
- team orientation to performance objectives such as achievement of goals, innovation, quality, customer service, and cost management
- co-operation – the willingness of team members to work with each other and to subordinate their own objectives and needs to those of their team
- flexibility – the willingness of team members to work flexibly in the interests of achieving team targets
- skill/competence acquisition – the need for team members to acquire the necessary skills and

competences to work well in a team environment (including the need for multi-skilling).

4   *Team objectives* – the types of objectives in the form of targets, standards, deadlines and budgets that could be set for teams.

5   *Team performance measures* – how the performance of the teams could be measured in relation to their objectives. Wherever possible, the aim should be to identify quantifiable measures of output, income, quality, customer service, etc.

6   *Employee opinion* – the opinions of line managers, team leaders and employees should be sounded out on whether or not team performance needs to be rewarded specifically and, if so, how. Employee opinions can be ascertained through an attitude survey, individual interviews or focus groups. The focus-group approach has much to commend it, especially if it covers a representative sample of employees and existing teams. The following are examples of the questions that could be put to focus groups:

- How important do you think good teamwork is in this organisation?
- Why do you think it is important?
- Do you believe that team members should be rewarded specifically for the achievements of their teams?
- If so, what sort of rewards do you think should be provided?
- What do you think would be the best basis for deciding on the scale of awards for teams?
- What do you think would be the fairest way of

distributing a team bonus among the team's members?
- Do you believe that it is right for individuals to be rewarded for their own performance, irrespective of that of their team?

Setting objectives for team pay

The initial analysis should provide the basis for deciding on whether or not to go ahead with team pay and, if so, for whom and in what form. It should also provide the background against which specific objectives for team pay can be set. These will provide guidelines on the design and implementation of the system and, importantly, on how its impact should be monitored and evaluated. The objectives can be defined in such areas as:

- improving the effectiveness of teamworking
- achieving measurable improvements in organisation performance through increased profit, productivity and quality, better customer service, innovation or cost control
- achieving cultural change – moving from an individualistic to a co-operative culture
- reflecting and reinforcing organisational changes to structure and process arising from delayering and/or an increased emphasis on lateral processes involving teamworking and project groups
- focusing the attention of teams on the organisation's critical success factors
- the basis upon which team pay should be financed – the aim should be to make it self-financing through productivity improvements and/or cost savings.

Consulting with and involving employees

The philosophy driving the development programme should be that 'people support what they help to create'. Team pay schemes must be 'felt fair' by those whom they affect, otherwise, like many of the original PRP schemes, they can work more as de-motivators than motivators.

Employees who will be affected by team pay should therefore be consulted on their reactions to it before development work starts. They should then be involved, as members of task forces, in designing the scheme, dealing with the objectives that might be set, the extent to which team members will take part in setting and agreeing those objectives, the bonus formula, how performance should be measured and the basis upon which team rewards should be distributed to team members.

Designing the scheme

Scheme design requires decisions to be made on the following elements of a team pay system:

- *Team eligibility* – which teams will be eligible for team pay, and why (specific team pay objectives may have to be set for different teams according to their type and purpose).
- *The quantitative measures or criteria* to be used for judging performance. These will vary according to the type of team. The criterion for a top management team may be improvements in any of the following: net profit, profitability, out-turn (however measured) or earnings per share. For a work team, depending on

the type of activity it carries out, the criteria could include such measures as output or sales figures, productivity, speed and accuracy of order processing, quality levels achieved, and customer satisfaction indices. The criterion for a project team could be completing the task to specification, on time and within the cost budget.

- *The qualitative criteria* which might be used to assess team performance, such as the quality of interpersonal relationships, co-operation within the team, and the relationship of the team with its internal and external customers.

- *The size of team bonuses* – this is a matter of judgement. As noted in Chapter 3, there are considerable variations, although according to Gross (1995): 'Conventional wisdom, which is always suspect, says that variable compensation, to be meaningful, needs to be about a month's pay...At minimum, it needs to be in the range of 5 per cent to 10 per cent of the base salary.' The amount made available will depend on the following factors:

  - a 'feel' for what a worthwhile payment will be in the particular organisation – this will represent the view of management on what size of bonus is required to provide an adequate incentive or reward and therefore to motivate team members
  - the degree of importance generally attached to financial rewards by the organisation and its members
  - policy on the proportion of total remuneration which it is believed should be at risk

- what the organisation believes it can afford to pay
  - this will be related to the extent to which the scheme is expected to be self-financing in terms of increased productivity or cost savings.

● The team pay formula – this establishes the relationship between team performance, as measured or assessed in quantitative or qualitative terms, and the reward. It also fixes the size of the bonus pool or fund earned by the team to be distributed among its members, or the scale of payments made to team members in relation to team performance against certain criteria. There are many methods of doing this.

  A bonus fund or pool may be appropriate when some flexibility is required in setting the level of payment to a team in relation to its performance and in distributing the sum among team members. The size of the fund allocated to a team may be based, as at Sun Life, on the cost savings generated by the team through increased productivity.

  The other approaches, as described in Chapter 3, include basing team bonus payments on:
  - performance related to defined criteria
  - an overall performance criterion
  - the achievement of team objectives.

● *Flexing team pay systems* – team pay systems are contingent on the type of team, and may be flexed for a team in its different stages of development. Organisational teams (eg top management) may have their team pay determined entirely by organisational performance. Business unit and departmental teams may be rewarded through a profit sharing or gain-sharing scheme. The bonus for work-based teams may take the form of one of the formulae mentioned above. Project teams are more likely to be awarded lump sums on the successful completion of the whole or part of a task.

Research conducted by Coil and Frohman (1994) established four stages of team development, and identified different types of reward for each stage as follows:

	Stage	Type of reward
1	Starting	Direction
2	Establishing	Support
3	Performing	Reinforcement
4	Ending	Celebration

Interestingly, it was concluded by Motorola that non-financial rewards at each stage were likely to be more effective than financial rewards.

- *Method of distribution* – the choice is between:

  - paying the same lump sum to all team members – this is the most even-handed approach, which assumes that each member makes the same level of contribution
  - dividing the team bonus fund among team members according to an assessment of their relative contribution – this could be regarded as the most equitable (using equity in the sense of rewarding individuals according to their just deserts) but it depends on assessments or ratings

that could be subjective or biased and therefore
potentially unfair
- allocating bonuses expressed as the same
percentage of basic pay for all team members – this
seems to be the most popular approach, perhaps
because it seems to take account of the
contribution of individual team members' level of
contribution, as long as their base pay properly
reflects that level.

A decision is also required on whether team pay
bonuses should be rigorously controlled from the
centre, thus ensuring uniformity, or whether some
degree of freedom should be devolved to team
leaders or self-managed teams to determine how
bonuses should be distributed. The latter approach
might not be favoured because it is subject to bias
and could result in inconsistent bonus payments.

● *Responsibility for directing and controlling team pay* – it is
advisable at the design stage to determine who is
going to be responsible for deciding on the size of
team bonus payments and how the scheme should
operate. Methods of monitoring and auditing the
scheme and evaluating its impact should also be
established. If team pay is to be related to cost
savings from productivity increases, the basis upon
which these would be measured has to be
determined.

Where schemes provide for team bonuses to be
linked to the achievement of team objectives,
arrangements need to be made on how the objectives
are set and agreed, and who is responsible for the

objective-setting process. It will be important to ensure that team objectives flow from organisational objectives and will support their achievement. Much better results will be achieved from the scheme if team members are involved in setting objectives and in agreeing on the measures that will be used to assess the team's performance.

- *Dealing with high and low individual performance in a team* – it is sometimes assumed by advocates of team pay that all members of a team contribute equally and should therefore be rewarded equally. In practice, the contribution of individual team members is likely to vary. When designing a team pay scheme, decisions have therefore to be made on the likelihood that some people will perform better or worse than others. It may be decided that even if this happens, it would be invidious and detrimental to single out individuals for different treatment. It may, however, be considered that 'special achievement' or 'sustained high performance' bonuses should be payable to individuals who make an exceptional contribution, while poor performers should receive a lower bonus or no bonus at all.

  If such a distinction is to be made, who makes it? Is it management on the basis of individual performance ratings made by team leaders? Is it the team leader who makes the recommendation? Or is it the team itself that proposes a differential payment? In the last case something may have to be done to prevent dominant individuals getting the prizes, or team members ganging up on their weaker brethren.

A variety of formal peer assessment or rating may be desirable to reduce the risk of prejudiced or unfair decisions being made. This could be backed up by guidelines on how ratings should be translated into bonus decisions. Proposals could be reviewed to ensure that these guidelines are followed and that recommendations do not appear to be unreasonable, bearing in mind that too much control from above might prejudice a desirable degree of autonomy. If individuals are to be rewarded, probably the best method is to provide for competency-related pay as well as team-based pay. Individual payments could be made as increases to the base rate, which would enhance the individual's team bonus if that were paid as a percentage of basic pay. Paying for individual competence *and* team performance is appealing because it seems to achieve the best of both worlds.

- *Project team bonuses* – the design considerations described above apply to permanent work teams. Different arrangements are required for project teams specially set up to achieve a task and, usually, disbanded after the task has been completed. Project team bonuses should, wherever possible, be self-financing – they should be related to increases in income or productivity, or cost savings arising from the project. Project teams can be set targets and their bonus can be linked to achieving or surpassing targeted results. Alternatively, a fixed bonus can be promised if the project is achieved on time, meets the specification and does not exceed the cost budget.

This bonus could be increased for early completion or to reflect cost savings. For lengthy projects, interim payments may be made at defined 'milestones'.

- Ad hoc *bonuses* – where there are no predetermined arrangements for paying bonuses to project teams, a retrospective bonus can be paid to a project or *ad hoc* team to recognise an exceptional achievement.

- *Team performance management* – the basis upon which the performance of teams should be measured and monitored by management and the teams themselves should be determined.

Introducing team pay

Team pay may be an unfamiliar device and it should therefore be introduced with care, especially if it is replacing an existing system of individual PRP. The process will work better if employees have been involved in developing the scheme, but it is still essential to communicate in detail to all employees the reasons for introducing team pay, how it will work and how it will affect them.

It is easier to introduce team pay into mature teams whose members are used to working together, trust one another and can recognise that team pay will work to their mutual advantage. Although it may seem an attractive proposition to use team pay as a means of welding new work teams together, there are dangers in forcing people who are already in a different situation to accept a radical change in their method of remuneration. It should be remembered that it may not be easy to get people in work teams to think of their performance in terms of how it impacts on others. It can take time for employees to adapt to a system in which a proportion of their pay is based on team achievement.

Clearly, this problem does not arise when teams are set up to tackle a special project. All the members of project or *ad hoc* teams know, or should know, that the project or task will be completed successfully only if they work well together.

When it comes to launching team pay it may be advisable to pilot it initially in one or two well-established teams. Experience gained from the pilot scheme can then be used to modify the scheme before it is extended elsewhere. If the pilot scheme teams think it has been a success, other teams may be more willing to convert to team pay.

Teambuilding and team leader training

Teambuilding training may be used to reinforce team pay (and *vice versa*) as part of the introduction programme. The training would aim to:

- increase awareness of the social processes that take place within teams
- develop the interactive or interpersonal skills that enable individuals to function well as team members
- increase the overall effectiveness of teamwork in the organisation.

Such teambuilding training could usefully be given to members of project teams.

Team leaders have an important role to play in making team pay a success. They should be given special training in how the scheme operates, and in their responsibilities for working with their teams in setting objectives, monitoring results, providing feedback and taking steps to improve performance.

Monitoring and evaluating team pay

Even when team pay has been planned and introduced carefully its success is not assured. It will be a new concept to most, if not all, of the people affected by it – team leaders as well as team members. Team pay should be closely monitored in its early stages and evaluated regularly to establish the extent to which it is achieving its aims and providing value for money.

Monitoring and evaluation processes should aim to find out:

- the extent to which team pay is achieving its objectives
- the opinions of line managers, team leaders and team members about team pay
- what improvements in performance have resulted from team pay
- what problems have been met
- how those concerned believe that these problems can be overcome.

A team pay audit should look at performance figures before and after the introduction of team pay and obtain the views of those involved through attitude surveys, individual interviews and focus groups.

Developing team pay

As reported by Caudron (1994), Trigon Blue Cross Shield established four cross-functional teams, all working together to service major clients. The plan for introducing team pay included the following steps:

- define the cross-functional teams
- define the business purpose and objectives of each team
- establish team performance measures
- train team members to work in a team environment
- establish the team performance review process
- develop an employee communication strategy
- define the funding base for the team incentive.

Potential problems

The problems of introducing team pay tend to relate to the identification and definition of teams, the choice of performance measures and the formula, the amount to be awarded and the basis of distribution. But other issues may have to be dealt with. When Kent County Council introduced team pay, as reported by IRS (1996a), the main drawbacks encountered were:

- failure to ensure that teams were defined clearly
- lack of commitment on the part of some team members
- lack of employee involvement in the design stage by imposing a pre-designed scheme
- lack of training and support for teams
- the time-consuming nature of agreeing team

accountabilities, setting targets, and monitoring and assessing performance.

These are fairly typical and can be addressed only by careful planning, involvement of team members in scheme design, the development and implementation of a communication strategy, the provision of team training, and providing guidance and support to teams in the processes of setting targets and monitoring performance. The action plan set out below spells out the main tasks to be accomplished when introducing team pay.

The team reward action plan

The following 12-point action plan summarises the approach to developing team reward processes that are most likely to be successful.

1 Assess the need for team rewards.
2 Find out if organisation is ready for team rewards.
3 Identify and define teams.
4 Set objectives.
5 Consult employees.
6 Consider options in conjunction with employees
   – team pay and/or other forms of team reward.
7 Design the team pay scheme in conjunction with employees, considering:
   – performance measures
   – the formula for linking performance to reward
   – the value of bonuses
   – the method of distribution to team members
   – rewards (if any) for individual contributions related to performance, skill or competence.

8 Communicate the details of the team pay scheme to employees.

9 Consider other methods of rewarding teams.

10 Conduct training in managing team rewards and in teambuilding.

11 Introduce team rewards.

12 Monitor and evaluate the team reward system.

How should team rewards be managed?

To manage team reward processes successfully it is necessary first to define the respective roles of management and teams; second, to decide on team performance measures; and third, to determine how they should be used.

The role of management

The role of management is to:

- conduct an initial analysis of the need for team pay and other forms of team reward
- analyse current practices to assess how team rewards might fit with them
- set objectives for team rewards
- define its philosophy on individual versus team rewards

- consider methods of reinforcing team pay or providing substitutes for it, such as gain-sharing
- decide how non-financial rewards (extrinsic and intrinsic) should be used either as an alternative to team pay or in conjunction with it
- create a collaborative climate in which management and employees jointly identify the need for team pay or other forms of team reward and develop team reward processes
- identify critical success factors for teams and consider how team behaviour needs to be modified
- develop a team reward system with the full involvement of line managers, team leaders, team members and their representatives
- communicate to employees the purpose of team rewards, how they function and the benefits they provide
- train team leaders and teams in defining their own critical success factors and in identifying performance measures
- train team leaders and teams in methods of measuring and assessing team performance and in the procedures for managing team pay
- provide teambuilding training for teams
- provide training and help with the implementation of personal development plans for team members to improve their skills and capabilities
- monitor and evaluate the implementation of team rewards to ensure that they function effectively
- audit the costs of team pay and take steps to make it self-financing, as far as this is possible

- promote the value of non-financial team rewards and train managers and team leaders in their use
- recognise team accomplishments by non-financial as well as financial means.

The role of teams

The role of teams is to:

- take part in the design and modification of the team pay system
- define team-critical success factors and performance measures
- set team objectives
- identify team accomplishments
- monitor and evaluate team performance generally and determine areas for improvement, especially in how the team functions
- establish priorities for team action in accordance with the criteria used in the team pay system
- analyse the financial rewards resulting from team pay and decide how they can be improved
- conduct, as appropriate, peer reviews of the performance of individual team members
- identify training and development needs for the team as a whole and its members, preparing team development plans and enlisting the support of management and specialist employee development staff in implementing the plans
- monitor the implementation of the team pay system and suggest improvements
- promote the use of non-financial rewards.

Although it is less usual, the team may take part in decisions on the distribution of team bonuses among its members.

The importance of monitoring and evaluation

Team pay may be worthwhile in the right circumstances but it is not an easy option, and team reward processes do not run themselves – they have to be managed. This means monitoring their effectiveness continuously and evaluating how well they contribute to team and organisational effectiveness against predetermined objectives. There will always be room for improvement.

Conclusions

Finally, it should be remembered that good teamwork may be enhanced by the reward system but there are other ways of developing it, as summarised in the following 10-point programme:

1 Describe and think of the organisation functioning as a set of processes carried out by interlocking teams united by a common purpose.

2 Devise and implement commitment and communications strategies that develop mutuality and identification with the organisation's goals and strategy.

3 Keep on emphasising that constructive teamwork is a key value in the organisation and ensure that the top management team practises what it preaches.

4 Ensure that the purpose and objectives of teams, and the basis upon which their performance will be measured, are clearly defined.

5 Create teams that are largely self-managed or self-directed, whose members jointly set their own specific short-term objectives within the framework of broader corporate and functional objectives, and define the measures they will use to monitor their own performance.

6 Take particular care over appointing and training team leaders. Emphasise that their role is to work alongside team members to achieve results by their collective efforts and to play a major part in developing the team as an effective unit.

7 Use team training to improve team processes, including setting objectives, planning, and monitoring performance as well as interpersonal skills.

8 Set overlapping or interlocking objectives for people who have to work together. These will take the form of targets to be achieved or projects to be completed by joint action.

9 Assess people's performance not only on the results they achieve but also on the degree to which they are effective team players.

10 Set up cross-functional project teams with a brief to get on with it.

References

ARMSTRONG M. *and* MURLIS H. (1998) *Reward Management*. 4th edn. London, Kogan Page.

ARMSTRONG M. *and* RYDEN O. (1996) *The IPD Guide on Team Reward*. London, Institute of Personnel and Development.

BECKHARD R. (1969) *Organisation Development: Strategy and models* Reading, Mass., Addison-Wesley.

CAUDRON S. (1994) 'Tie individual pay to team success'. *Personnel Journal*. October. pp40–46.

COIL M. *and* FROHMAN M. (1994) *Motorola Team Research Project*. Unpublished.

GILES L., KODZ J. *and* EVANS C. (1997) *Productive Skills for Process Operatives*. IES Report 336. London, Institute of Employment Studies.

GROSS S. (1995) *Compensation for Teams*. New York, American Management Association.

INCOMES DATA SERVICES (1993) 'Managers, teams and reward'. *IDS Management Pay Review*. August. pp20–23.

INCOMES DATA SERVICES (1996) 'Team bonuses at Bradford & Bingley'. *IDS Management Pay Review*. May. pp2–5.

INDUSTRIAL RELATIONS SERVICES (1995) 'Key issues in team working'. *Employee Development Bulletin*. No.69. September. pp5–15.

INDUSTRIAL RELATIONS SERVICES (1996a) 'Team reward: part 2'. *Pay and Benefits Bulletin*. March. pp2–8.

INDUSTRIAL RELATIONS SERVICES (1996b) 'Gainsharing at BP Exploration'. *Pay and Benefits Bulletin*. No.393. February. pp6–9.

INDUSTRIAL RELATIONS SERVICES (1997a) 'New reward practices in the USA'. *Pay and Benefits Bulletin*. October. pp2–9.

INDUSTRIAL RELATIONS SERVICES (1997b) 'Sharing the gains at Rank Xerox'. *Pay and Benefits Bulletin*. No.431. September. pp4–9.

INDUSTRIAL RELATIONS SERVICES (1998) 'HR change at British Steel: a cast-iron success story'. *Pay and Benefits Bulletin*. No.655. May. pp.11–16.

INDUSTRIAL RELATIONS SERVICES (1999) 'Pay prospects for 2000'. *Pay and Benefits Bulletin*. No.483. November. pp4–13.

JOHNSON S. T. (1996) 'One firm's approach to team incentive pay'. *Compensation and Benefits Review*. September–October. pp47–50.

KATZENBACH J. *and* SMITH D. (1993) *The Magic of Teams*. Boston, Mass., Harvard Business School Press.

KINNIE N. *and* PURCELL J. (1998) 'Side effects'. *People Management*. 30 April. pp34–6.

KINNIE N., HUTCHINSON S. *and* PURCELL J. (1998) *Getting Fit, Staying Fit: Developing lean and responsive organisations*. London, Institute of Personnel and Development.

LAWLER E. E. (1971) *Pay and Organisational Effectiveness*. New York, McGraw Hill.

LAWLER E. E. (1997) 'Tricky but not impossible'. *Across the Board*. February. pp20–21.

MOHRMAN A. M. *and* MOHRMAN S. A. (1995) 'Performance management is "running the business"'. *Compensation and Benefits Review*. July–August. pp69–75.

PASCARELLA P. (1997) 'Compensation for teams'. *Across the Board*. February. pp16–22.

SLATER J. A. *and* WEST M. A. (1995) 'Satisfaction or source of pressure: the paradox of teamwork'. *The Occupational Psychologist*. April. pp30–34.

THOMPSON M. (1995) *Team Working and Pay*. Brighton, The Institute of Employment Studies.

WEST M. A. *and* SLATER J. A. (1995) 'Teamwork: myths, realities and research'. *The Occupational Psychologist*. April. pp24–9.